Mellifluous

Corin Peters

BookLeaf Publishing

Presentation by *BookLeaf Publishing*

Web: www.bookleafpub.com

E-mail: info@bookleafpub.com

ISBN: 9789357213554

First edition 2023

lovely bodies

It always starts with the hands
reaching out to touch, a cheek, through hair,
acting like lips.
Quivering please - let me join.
Then your hands, throw flowers,
covering a night in petals,
little kisses rain down.
Catch them, catch a moment
catch the look.
Feeling through the dark, finding
the valley of a body,
inseparable, grateful to touch,
beautiful, to be human.

gaze

I see you over there,
Under the moonlit sky,
With stars in your hair,
They shine through your eyes.

You may as well have been,
A million miles away,
For my love will remain secret,
Not to be revealed today.

previous nights

3

Morning came strong and unforgiving,
like a mountain full of light,
reigning and dominant on the valley below.
As you rolled around
not shaking the days hand,
spiteful.

Mouth as dry as a desert
full of flies, speaking for you,
like little demons.
Spreading anxiety
through blood and brain.

Last night follows like a tail
wagging affirmation and approval,
predatory animal.

Brush your teeth,
brush away sand,
brush away wine,
like a god,
last night's triumph.

Night returns full of laughter,
eyes watering wind,

outside smoking and locking eyes,
creating clouds, with all.

Then like ants scattered
and orderly,
touching antennas
and talking.
you look lovely
you look lovely,
I want to cry.

While drifting through smoke,
through smiles,
a hungry room devours,
home in the indigo night,
home in the flowers.

november thirteen

5

Eggs for breakfast,
sunlight for lunch,
a break from reality,
a wine.
Love for dinner,
the moon and I.
Light, intertwined.

deluge of the heart

6

In rains company,
alone with a cup of coffee,
or was it tea?
It does not belong to me,
it is empty.

I watch drop by drop,
rain falling from above,
plop, plop!
It is overflowing, my love.

grace

Every step you take
the earth trembles,
with envy.
Mountains crumble,
at mercy,
forests bloom,
garlands of flowers
admiring you,
It's no contest
whose beauty towers.

prelude

8

If I stepped out,
of my world,
into yours,
for a brief encounter,
would I be welcome,
would we smile,
warm hands to hold you,
to silence our world,
for a little while.

dream jar

She permeates my dreams,
like light,
in a windowed room.
Surrounding all with warmth,
for the indoor plant, death.

For in my dreams, she won't
lock eyes to mine.
Holding me prison - to anticipation,
all the while,
lighting my world,
with fire.

distance

My mind was as empty as night
and full of sky,
Until the same stars
that lived in my dreams,
appeared in your eyes,
I lost all sense and
started to wonder,
while I wandered,
what was filling my sky now.
It was the same stars,
only fire and light, above,
speaking differently,
exploding with love.
If time allows
I hope it is kind,
to meet you again,
arms made of hearts,
open wide.

poetic entanglement

I can't carry you forever
book of poetry,
for you wither
and you remind me,
of my inevitable withering.
As time eats away,
the pages of my days.

But I will hold on,
if I can hold things,
as the fruit holds onto
branches - branches to leaves,
tattoo to skin,
I will hold you, my love.
For in you,
my soul is written,
and my mind is
tattooed on your pages.

dusk

12

Evening didn't wait for us,
the world continued turning,
birds made blankets of the sky
and we blanketed our eyes,
as we slept.
Where from time,
we felt safe,
we hid from change,
freezing love overnight,
leaving no trace.

ladder of light

13

In the caves of
our minds,
dark recesses - danger
in corridors,
navigate with care,
with love.
Search for doors,
made of starlight,
there's beauty
in every corner,
even webs
glisten in the sun.

singularity

White rose,
garden of green,
star in the sky,
lone night cigarette,
the dot on the i
c'est moi,
a glowing song,
singing rivers,
alone and lovely.

one second

In the hour of the star,
chime of a clock,
page of a book,
time presents itself, from afar.

Precious like a gem,
calming as the wind.
Genderless! Timeless!
Unified!

Around every corner,
in the eye of the lover,
a salad of seconds,
the latter and the former.

I love you, oh moment
I miss you, it passes
I need you, tangible.

Hidden, life like a meaning,
in your dreams,
like a feeling.
Without you,
time goes along,
like a love.

mirage

Her name,
pretty like fruit,
eating tomatoes whole,
like grapes.
She would gather flowers,
place them in the bathroom,
filling the sink with grass,
the toilet,
with tulips,
fighting with time,
finding her name,
climbing tears
to a reality.

piece of the moon

To crave memory is to crave death - it only
happens once.
At once eternal, wind in space.
Nobody sees it coming, no angle of advantage,
even from yourself.
You can't wrestle that which happens to all
living beings.
You can't wrestle love from a being - squish the
plant to death!
Starve the love forth, to feed you another day.
Prolong is an antidote, in any language,
prolong that which makes you feel, until your
hunger is satisfied.
Prolong the moment, forests of memories,
forests of life, full of creatures you have named -
leaves being born from the sun of your mind.
Sleep in the shade of this prolonged field of love
until you're born again.
Entangled in the poetry of your submission.
Grow and glow your palms, so you can hold all
life within your fingers, hold tight all that you've
felt.
Adore all that you feel.
Use this when your hair is grey,
use this when the wind blows in circles,

throws stones into space and scatters dirt over
cities.
Hurling waste into gardens and plates of food.
Use it to calm your mind, while the earth rotates
around your mind.
Give in to the act of love, give in to giving love -
everything craves it and its free.
As is hate, hate not giving love.
Love writing a letter about love,
love your hands for writing a letter,
love your mind for letting your hands write a
letter,
I love you.
Love the flowers that follow you, give them
permission to bloom.
Don't decide on their colours, the bee's
master-craft.
Let them ask to be in a vase, ask to be in your
hair, beautiful.
Let the caterpillars glide through your hair, like
rope climbers,
adventuring over your body, its chasms, its
lakes, the abyss,
creating a path of travel, full of life, full of love.

Run, when you can - hair flowing like fire, until
there's tears in your eyes,
creating rivers of your thoughts.

Let gravity take these pools into the soil, to give
dreams to grass,
colour the dirt gold - like a family.
Fall, when you can - pebble into a pond, fall into
the depths,
eyes closed until you become a shadow, let the
shadow whisper air
into you, a warm air, rumbling your being until
you are still, like space.
As light shines down through the surface, stars
start to rescue you, they
fall in the millions - leaving enough to stay.
They light up everything around you, like a
million lamps - you're becoming
one of them, floating in space, shining like the
sky at night.
Observe yourself, lovely from afar.
As you descend, growing complete - taking bits
of stars with you, a portion of a planet, a piece of
the moon.
Awake, a child of air, open and cry, because you
can.
A child born of the universe, in your eyes; dust
from a widowed planet,
in your heart; birth of a new galaxy, your voice;
a supernova,
your hair; the comets tail - limitless fire.

the author

Where does your thought start?
beginning a form - like a paintbrush
on a naked landscape.
Are you mellow with the first stroke?
melancholy water blue,
a fluid sky peppered with clouds,
seasoning your art,
colouring your letters.

Nonetheless,
I eat your words,
like a savage beast,
hungry for love.
I read in the infinite,
such graceful idioms,
you're speaking to me
and I love you too.

fluidity

Don't fall for love,
you will eat anything
when hungry.
Even words,
tripping over them, like
fallen trees.
Tread as if you were walking
through water, tread slowly
as if the fish were speaking
to your ankles, words of promise,
of love.
Answer with a step, forward and slow,
soon they'll forget you were
ever there, you don't remember reality
when you dream.
Life is like that,
beautiful images of a lie.
Like a mirror, showing you
a reflection unrecognisable.
Like a shadow,
a trick of the light.

bite of life

Fear has no substance,
like a dream, real at eyes closed,
forgotten with dawn.
A hand more stained,
from letters, from touch
battered by experience.
While the other,
clean and pure,
living in solitude,
like an egg.
We all perish in the sun of life,
we are not incapable of love -
you can't hold love like a bird.
Deliverance is our reply.

dawn of colour

Disillusionment
starts to ooze,
the minds canvas,
inevitable aptitude.

The window of my eye
became,
like paint falling,
wine red; honey yellow; star-light,
dawning.

My kaleidoscope vision,
sky melting gold,
while trees bled
to indigo in the night,
brown hair now fire red.

Clouds to charcoal,
and moths – doomed,
following the flame,
instead of the moon.

first letter

Although brief,
No less beautiful.
Our time slowed down,
With care.

I am thankful,
Thoughtful of when,
My memory will hold you,
Until then.

My heart will hold, only joy.
My mind a garden,
For your flowers,
Growing love.

www.ingramcontent.com/pod-product-compliance
Lightning Source LLC
Chambersburg PA
CBHW070735160726
48003CB00006BA/2515